"I WAS ALWAYS LOOKING OUTSIDE MYSELF FOR STRENGTH AND CONFIDENCE BUT IT COMES FROM WITHIN. IT IS THERE ALL THE TIME."

~ ANNE FREUD

TO LISA BILYEU - WHOSE LIFE-CHANGING BOOK
"RADICAL CONFIDENCE" INSPIRED ME TO WRITE
ABOUT BECOMING & BEING
THE HERO OF OUR OWN LIVES

THE GIRL THAT MAKES MISTAKES
Published by LHC Publishing 2023

Text Copyright © 2023 Y. Eevi Jones
Illustrations Copyright © 2023 Y. Eevi Jones

Printed in the USA.

All the characters in this book are fictitious, and any resemblance to actual persons living or dead is purely coincidental.

All rights reserved. No part of this publication may be reproduced, distributed, or transmitted in any form or by any means, or stored in a database or retrieval system, without the prior written permission of the copyright holder.

All inquiries should be directed to
www.LHCpublishing.com

ISBN-13: 978-1-952517-22-8 Paperback
ISBN-13: 978-1-952517-23-5 Hardcover

THE GIRL THAT MAKES MISTAKES

GROWING CONFIDENCE
ONE DAY AT A TIME

EEVI JONES

I'M THE GIRL THAT MAKES MISTAKES,
MISTAKES THAT LEAD TO GROWTH.
I'M THE GIRL THAT WINS AND FAILS,
FOR REACHING DREAMS REQUIRES BOTH.

GETTING BIGGER, BETTER, BOLDER;
THAT'S WHAT GROWTH IS ALL ABOUT.
A PURSUIT THAT'S NEVER ENDING,
FOR TRUE GROWTH CAN'T BE WITHOUT.

GROWTH REQUIRES CHANGE.
IT'S A THIRST AND QUEST FOR MORE.
GROWTH VENTURES ALONG WINDING PATHS
NEVER EXPLORED BEFORE.

GROWTH IS SLOW. IT'S HARD. IT'S SCARY.
BUT NECESSARY NONETHELESS.
WHERE MY INNER NOS AND MAYBES
MUST FIRST BECOME A YES.

A YES TO DREAM AUDACIOUSLY,
WHERE I ALONE DEFINE MY WEALTH.
A YES TO SHOW UP EVERY DAY,
BELIEVING IN MYSELF.

WITH GROWTH I'VE COME TO UNDERSTAND
THAT I CAN DO HARD THINGS.
WHEN FAILING, I CAN TRY AGAIN,
NO MATTER WHAT LIFE BRINGS.

FOR LIFE IS FULL OF HIGHS AND LOWS,
BUT NONE OF THEM WILL LAST.
SO WHILE FULLY LIVING MY BEST **TODAYS**,
MY **BEFORES** STAY IN THE PAST.

I CAN'T CHANGE WHAT HAS ALREADY BEEN.
I CAN ONLY CHANGE WHAT IS.
MY TODAYS AND MY TOMORROWS BRING
ALL THAT I DO NOT WANT TO MISS.

BECAUSE EVERY MOMENT IN OUR LIFE
IS A FUTURE MEMORY.
AND HOW I WILL REMEMBER IT
IS COMPLETELY UP TO ME.

WHEN UPSET, I MAY FEEL ANGRY.
WHEN LET DOWN, I MAY FEEL SAD.
WHEN CONFUSED, I MAY FEEL LOST.
WHEN HURT, I MAY GET MAD.

BUT EMOTIONS - THEY'RE JUST TOOLS
THAT MEASURE HOW I FEEL.
AND LETTING THEM TAKE OVER
WON'T FIX WHAT NEEDS TO HEAL.

SO I FEEL THE FEELS, BUT THEN LET GO,
KNOWING THAT THIS TOO SHALL PASS.
FOR EMOTIONS, UNLIKE DIAMONDS,
ARE NOT FOREVER AND WON'T LAST.

WE SO OFTEN CONFUSE WHO WE ARE
WITH WHAT WE DO IN LIFE.
WE SO OFTEN MAKE OTHERS THE SOURCE
FROM WHICH ALL OUR POWERS DERIVE.

BUT WHAT DEFINES MY WORTH
SHOULD COME FROM ME ALONE.
WHERE SELF-LOVE AND SELF-COMPASSION
HAVE CREATED A JUDGMENT-FREE ZONE.

Where I'm inspired by others' successes.
Where I'm encouraged to see others win.
'Cause seeing others slaying their day
Stirs my own roaring powers within.

Roaring powers that make me believe
Any dream of mine can be reached.
Roaring powers that urge me to leap
Even before the trust in myself is fully unleashed.

CONFIDENCE IS SUCH A BIG WORD,
WHEN IT'S REALLY JUST A MEANS
TO HOLD MY GROUND, NO MATTER HOW
IMPOSSIBLE IT SEEMS.

CONFIDENCE IS A BELIEF,
WHERE DESPITE NOT KNOWING HOW,
I'M WILLING TO JUST TRY.
NOT LATER, BUT RIGHT NOW.

PERHAPS IT WON'T BE PERFECT.
PERHAPS IT WON'T BE RIGHT.
BUT THAT'S OKAY, AS LONG AS I
BELIEVED I CAN AND TRIED.

BECAUSE CONFIDENCE IS CREATED,
WHEN I ALLOW MYSELF TO FAIL.
WHEN ON MY WAY THROUGH SOARING SKIES
MISTAKES WON'T BREAK MY SAIL.

FOR IF I FAILED A THOUSAND TIMES,
BUT TRIED AGAIN AND DIDN'T QUIT,
I'VE SIMPLY FOUND A THOUSAND WAYS
TO SHOW MY BOLD AND GRIT.

Confidence is not the goal.
It's what grows and blossoms along the way,
when despite my fears and doubts,
I do it anyway.

For I only do something for the first time once.
So I don't fear to face the new.
'Cause with each time that follows the first,
I get better at whatever I do.

FAILING DOESN'T MAKE ME A FAILURE,
BECAUSE EACH TRY IS BETTER THAN NONE.
BEING WILLING TO GROW WEIGHS OUNCES,
WHILE NOT TRYING WEIGHS A WHOLE TON.

NEITHER SUCCESS NOR FAILURE
DEFINE WHO I AM WITHIN.
AS LONG AS I LEARN FROM WHAT I DO,
IT'S A BIG AND MIGHTY WIN.

So I'm the girl that gets back up.
I'm the girl that tries again.
And when the tough's staring at my face,
I remember who I am.

I'M THE GIRL THAT'S NOT AFRAID
TO MAKE MISTAKES, TO GROW AND THRIVE.
FOR THROUGH MY BRAVE I'VE COME TO BE
THE HERO OF MY OWN LIFE.

THE END.

ABOUT THE AUTHOR

Writing under a number of pen names, Eevi Jones is a *USA Today* & *WSJ* bestselling and award-winning author and ghostwriter of children's books.

Born in former East Germany to a German mother and a Vietnamese father, Eevi loves to infuse her children's books with racial diversity. She is the founder of *Children's Book University*® where dreams really do come true. *The Girl That Makes Mistakes* is Eevi's first book specifically written for young adults.

Eevi has been featured in *Forbes*, *Scary Mommy*, *Business Insider*, *Huffington Post*, *Exceptional Parent Magazine*, and more.

She can be found online at www.BravingTheWorldBooks.com.

A WORD BY THE AUTHOR

I hope that with this book you come to see how special you truly are, and what incredible powers every single one of us holds within. How we perceive the world around us is ALWAYS up to us! We are the heroes of our own lives!

If you enjoyed this book, it would mean the world to me if you would take a short minute to leave a heartfelt review. Thank you.

OTHER WORKS BY THIS AUTHOR

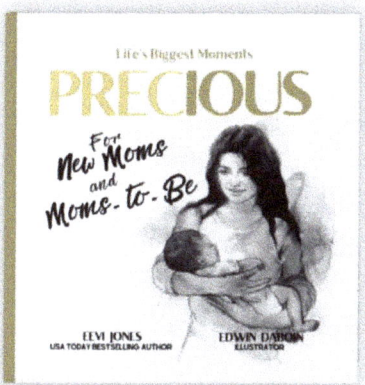

... AND MANY MORE

www.ingramcontent.com/pod-product-compliance
Lightning Source LLC
Chambersburg PA
CBHW041231240426
43673CB00010B/302